The World of Work

Choosing a Career in Transportation

Most people rely on some form of transportation to get them from place to place.

The World of Work
Choosing a Career in Transportation

by Bruce McGlothlin

THE ROSEN PUBLISHING GROUP, INC.
NEW YORK, NY

Published in 1997 by The Rosen Publishing Group, Inc.
29 East 21st Street, New York, NY 10010

First Edition

Library of Congress Cataloging-in-Publication Data

McGlothlin, Bruce.
    Choosing a career in transportation/Bruce McGlothlin.
       p.   cm.—(The world of work)
    Includes bibliographical references and index.
    ISBN   0-8239-2278-2
    1. Transportation—Vocational guidance—United States. I. Title.
II. Series.
HE203.M33   1996
388′.023′73—dc20   96-9454
                                                    CIP
                                                    AC

Manufactured in the United States of America

Contents

Introduction

Have you ever dreamed of driving an eighteen-wheel rig across the country? Or perhaps you see yourself as a busy flight attendant serving passengers aboard an airplane bound for Europe. Or maybe you picture yourself working on the engine of a bus, car, truck, or boat? Could you be the one flying a plane, operating a train, or driving a limousine?

All of these jobs are part of the exciting nonstop world of the *transportation industry*. These jobs offer a sense of power, responsibility, and independence. They also provide variety, challenges, and the opportunity to have a successful career. Doing something you enjoy and getting a chance to see the country or the world are only part of the benefits of a career in transportation.

Our world is developing at a fast pace. Much of the remarkable progress is due to the transportation industry. Cars, boats, trains

Many long-haul truck drivers begin their careers by working for a variety of shipping companies.

airplanes, and buses are constantly being improved. This adds to the speed and efficiency of transporting goods and people.

This is happening throughout the United States and the world. Modern transportation links countries together in a matter of hours and minutes rather than days and weeks.

Transportation is considered a *service industry*. This means that it helps move people and goods from one place to another quickly, efficiently, and cheaply. Transportation is vital to most countries. Without it, goods and services could not be delivered or produced. People could not travel to their jobs or destinations. Transportation careers operate at all times throughout the world.

Bob, Truck Driver

Bob liked all types of vehicles and considered becoming a truck or limousine driver in the future. At a career day at school, he listed transportation as a possible career choice.

His school guidance counselor placed him in a group to meet with John Hobbs, the state director of transportation services. Mr. Hobbs described many types of transportation careers. He also discussed the personal traits and abilities needed to be successful.

Generally, people in the transportation field

must have good eyesight and coordination and be in good physical condition. They need patience, good judgment, and the ability to work well under pressure. They must be neat and clean and have good clerical skills and mechanical problem-solving abilities.

Above all, Mr. Hobbs told students that people in the field of transportation must have a strong desire to help and serve people.

Bob learned that a college degree was not necessary to enter the transportation industry. Many jobs required some education. Others offered on-the-job training. Some careers, such as administrative and specialized positions, did require a college degree. Bob thought these jobs might be future possibilities.

Questions to Ask Yourself
The transportation industry offers many exciting opportunities for those who are motivated and are willing to work hard. 1) What type of transportation career would best suit your interests, talents, and abilities? 2) What careers require a high school diploma? 3) Who can help you in planning your career?

Job opportunities in the airline industry range from baggage handler to pilot.

Careers in the Airline Industry

1

Pete, Baggage Handler

Pete had always wanted to pursue an airline career. He wanted a job where he could travel. But airline jobs were tough to find.

One day, Pete saw an ad in the paper for baggage handlers with a new airline. He visited the employment office of the airline and applied for the job. Within a week, he was interviewed and given the job. This was the first step toward Pete's dream career.

During the first few months, Pete discovered many new things. His main job was to transfer baggage from incoming planes to the baggage claim area. He also helped load baggage onto planes when needed. He learned to operate baggage trucks and fork lifts. For this work, Pete needed to have his high school diploma and a driver's license.

As his experience increased, Pete discovered a variety of airline jobs that he qualified for by having his high school diploma. Some jobs required college courses or training. The airline paid for its employees to take college courses, so Pete thought about signing up for a few courses. He liked the idea of working his way up.

Most of the *service jobs* at an airport and most jobs with airlines are union jobs. This means that the terms of the job are negotiated and protected by a *labor union.* *Wages* for a *baggage handler* start at $10 an hour. The wage increases as a person's abilities and skill levels increase. Airlines usually offer *benefits* to all employees. These may include health and life insurance, and paid vacation and sick days. Most employees are allowed to join the airline's retirement plan.

To advance, employees can apply for other jobs they are qualified for based on education, experience, and seniority. One great benefit for all airline employees is the stand-by traveling status. That means that an employee and his immediate family can travel anywhere in the world for free when empty seats on the flight are available.

Baggage handlers earn tips as well as a salary.

Jeanne, Pilot

Jeanne had dreamed of becoming a pilot since grade school. She imagined herself flying around the world in a jumbo jet. This was a job that offered everything she ever wanted—responsibility, freedom, and money.

In high school, Jeanne began to research her career. She discovered that pilots fly airplanes and helicopters. She learned that many pilots begin their careers as flight engineers. Then they become copilots, and finally pilots.

Pilots must learn everything about the working system of an aircraft. Besides flying, they are responsible for take-offs and landings. Both can be difficult at times in certain weather conditions. They perform safety checks and maintain the high safety standards set by the Federal Aviaton Administration (FAA).

Nonflying duties include supervising the boarding and unboarding of passengers, refueling, keeping flight records, scheduling flights, and coordinating all members of the flight and ground crew.

The more Jeanne learned about being a pilot, the more certain she was that she was making the right choice.

Job opportunities for *pilots*, *copilots*, and *flight engineers* are very competitive. Many airlines prefer to hire pilots with college degrees and military flight experience. Pilots must be in good health. They must also have a *pilot's license*. This is earned by passing written, physical, and flight exams given by the FAA. A pilot must also have several years of experience in working with the aircraft that he or she will fly.

Pilots can earn high *salaries*. Airline pilots or *captains* earn $70,000 to $80,000 a year. Copilots earn $40,000 to $50,000, while flight engineers earn $30,000 to $40,000.

There are many different types of airplanes. Some, such as seaplanes, are designed to land on water.

In addition to working for airlines, pilots work for corporations. They also work in specialized areas such as crop dusting, seed planting, fire fighting, law enforcement, traffic monitoring, and rescue and hospital evacuation.

One way to become a pilot is to join a college program that offers the opportunity to obtain a private pilot's license. Another way is to join one of the armed forces, such as the Air Force. You have to choose the path that fits your skills and abilities.

Other Careers in the Airline Industry

Airline flight attendants provide comfort and safety to passengers. They are trained to follow strict rules to ensure the safety of the crew and passengers during the flight or during any emergency situation. Attendants may also serve food and beverages during flights. To be a flight attendant, some college experience is preferred. Specialized schooling for three to six months is provided by the airline. The salary range is between $13,000 and $20,000.

Airline ticket agents get people and luggage to the right place at the right time for flights. They sell tickets, give flight information, and check luggage onto flights.

Airline ticket agents receive *on-the-job* training. However, a high school diploma is required and some college experience may be preferred. Good clerical and people skills are also needed. The salary range is $15,000 to $25,000 a year.

Airline dispatchers schedule flights for an airline. They make certain all FAA rules are followed. Dispatchers are in constant contact with pilots about the weather, landings, take-offs, schedules, flight plans, and maintenance of the aircrafts.

Some college experience and flight knowledge is preferred when applying for a dispatcher position. The salary range is $20,000 to $30,000 a year.

Airline mechanics maintain and service all aircrafts owned by the airline. They repair, service, and inspect airplanes for airlines, private corporations, and the military.

A thorough knowledge and understanding of all aircraft engines and systems is required to be an airline mechanic. Specialized training in airplane mechanics is necessary to receive an aircraft mechanic's license. There are one and two year programs at technical and aircraft schools that offer programs for aircraft mechanics. The salary range is $25,000 to $40,000 a year.

Air traffic controllers ensure the safety of each flight in the air. They make sure that planes don't collide when they take off, fly, or land. Air traffic controllers coordinate and track flights on radar screens within a certain area. This job can be stressful because of the huge responsibility of ensuring the safety of others.

To be an air traffic controller, college experience is required, as well as specialized training. This is a job with the federal government. It is on *civil service listings*. This means that you must take an exam offered by the government to apply for this job. The salary range starts between $25,000 and $30,000. If you are interested in this job, go to your nearest civil service agency to register for a civil service test.

Radio operators operate, maintain, and repair radios on aircrafts and at terminals.

A high school diploma is required to become a radio operator. Specialized training in electronics or radio repair is preferred. Most jobs require employees to pass special FAA licensing exams. The salary range is $20,000 to $30,000. The best way to begin this career is to look for specialized training schools in radio repair or electronics.

Questions to Ask Yourself

There are many exciting opportunities within the airline industry. 1) What type of airline career interests you? Why? 2) How can you prepare yourself for an airline career? 3) How can you learn what airline jobs might be available in your area?

Careers in the Railroad Industry

2

The loud, high-pitched sound of the whistle and the rumbling sound of moving cars signal something thrilling to people who work in the railroad industry. Many have loved train travel since they were children playing with model trains.

Peyton, Future Conductor

Since he was a child, Peyton loved to play with model trains. As he grew older, the sight, sound, and smell of trains continued to fascinate him.

Peyton was a good mechanic. But he didn't want to operate or fix engines. He just liked to ride on trains. Peyton had good organizational and clerical skills. He enjoyed being around and working with people. One day, someone suggested that Peyton look into becoming a railroad conductor. Peyton decided that was a great idea.

To many people, trains represent the excitement of travel and adventure.

Conductors do a variety of jobs. They are responsible for the general safety of passengers, crew, and freight aboard the train. They usually inspect each train car and supervise any repairs done during their trip. Conductors collect fares and tickets, and provide information to passengers.

Conductors must keep accurate records about each trip. Good clerical and people skills are necessary to deal with both passengers and the crew in a friendly and helpful way. Conductors must know the signals, train schedules, and company rules.

Railroad conductors usually begin their careers as *brakemen*. Brakemen operate and repair brake systems. Good mechanical skills are necessary. The salary range is $30,000 to $40,000 a year.

Promotions are based on the *seniority* system. This means that people who have worked there the longest have the best chance for promotion to new positions. High school graduates with good mechanical, organizational, and clerical skills have the best chance for moving up the career ladder.

Once you have a job with a railroad, you must join a labor union. Unions negotiate salaries, hours, and benefits for railroad workers. Most railroad workers receive benefits such as health and life insurance and retirement plans. Some may also receive paid sick and vacation days. Once you are a member of a union, it is easier to move up the career ladder since jobs usually go to union members first.

Unfortunately, because more people are flying rather than taking the train, railroads are cutting back services. However, there are jobs available. And for some people, trains are the best place to be.

Other Careers in the Railroad Industry

Most jobs in the railroad industry require a high school diploma. They also require employees to have good mechanical, people, and clerical skills.

Railroad engineers usually operate diesel engines that pull both freight and passenger trains locally and across the country.

Engineers must understand how the diesel engine works. They must also be able to make minor repairs to trains in the rail yard. They move passenger and freight cars to the rail yard before and after a trip or run. They are responsible for regular inspections of the train's mechanical parts. An engineer needs to understand track operating rules and signals.

Engineers often begin their careers as firemen. *Firemen* assist in the safe operation of the train, acting as assistant engineers. Many firemen go on to enter engineer training programs to become railroad engineers.

Engineers and firemen receive on-the-job training as well as classroom instruction. Learning standard procedures and company rules and regulations is essential to safely operate a train.

To become an engineer or fireman, it is necessary to have a high school diploma. You must also be between the ages of 18 and 35. The salary range for engineers is $50,000 to $60,000 a year. For firemen the range is $30,000 to $40,000 a year.

Working hours vary from forty to sixty hours a week. Engineers and firemen are often *on call*. This means that they could be called back to work from home if they are needed. Maintaining good physical strength and endurance is important since these jobs are physically demanding.

Railroad brake, signal, and *switch operators*

You must be strong, clever, and enjoy working outdoors to be a railroad maintenance worker.

use, maintain, and repair brakes, signals, and switches that are required for the safe and efficient operation of trains. These workers must have excellent mechanical skills and physical strength. Training is usually on-the-job. The salary range is $20,000 to $30,000 a year.

Railroad maintenance workers keep trains, engines, and equipment in good working shape. These jobs include: car repairers, machinists, boilermakers, electrical workers, sheet metal workers, and blacksmiths. Each job has different levels of technical training.

Railroad maintenance workers must have excellent mechanical skills, as well as physical strength and endurance. The salary range is $20,000 to $30,000 a year.

Track maintenance workers maintain and repair rails and track beds to keep trains moving. Most of this work is done outside, which means working in all kinds of weather. Physical strength and endurance are essential.

Having a high school diploma is preferred for track maintenance workers. On-the-job training is provided. The salary range is $15,000 to $20,000 a year.

Railroad telegraphers and *telephone* and *tower operators* are responsible for the maintenance, repair, and operation of the communication systems between trains and stations.

For these jobs, high school graduates with some technical, computer, communication, or electrical training are preferred. The salary range is $25,000 to $35,000 a year.

Railroad station ticket agents sell tickets, maintain records, check baggage, and provide information to passengers.

Some college experience may be helpful in becoming a ticket agent. Good clerical and people skills are necessary. The salary range is $20,000 to $30,000 a year.

Questions to Ask Yourself

Perhaps train travel has always interested you. Here are some things to think about. 1) What type of railroad career is appealing to you? 2) How can you learn more about that job? 3) Why have the career opportunities in the railroad industry become limited? What does this mean for you?

Careers in the Trucking Industry

3

Have you ever wanted to drive across the country? Or perhaps you like the idea of driving a large local delivery truck. Or maybe you'd like to be the one who sends the trucks out on their jobs.

The trucking industry is one of the few industries in the field of transportation where a person can be his or her own boss. For instance, you can own your own long-haul truck or your own moving company.

Joe, Truck Driver

Joe loved to drive and work on cars in his spare time. After he graduated from high school, he wanted to become a truck driver. Maybe it was the size of the truck or its powerful engine. Perhaps it was the sense of freedom and independence he felt whenever he drove.

Joe's goal was to own his own truck, or rig. He wanted to haul freight on cross-country trips. In talking with different truckers who owned their own rigs, he learned it would cost a lot of money to buy a rig.

Joe decided to work until he could save enough money. For several months, he drove a construction dump truck. This job was a valuable experience for two reasons. He earned a good salary. His salary range was $17,000 to $25,000 a year. Health and life insurance and retirement benefits were included. And he learned to operate a large truck.

After this job, Joe worked for a snack company. Every day he delivered snacks to local convenience stores. This was good work because it gave him the chance to meet a lot of people. It also gave him experience with driving a truck in city traffic.

Several months later, Joe began to think about his dream career of driving his own rig. It was then that he decided to apply for a job at various trucking companies. This would allow him to gain experience and earn enough money to buy his own rig.

Long haul truck drivers drive trucks carrying freight from one place to another. They often travel long distances in short periods of time.

In order to operate a *rig*, or an eighteen-

Many truck drivers own their own rigs.

wheel truck, a driver must have a special state-issued chauffeur's license. You can learn the requirements for such a license by calling your local Department of Motor Vehicles.

The United States Department of Transportation sets the minimum requirements for long-haul truck drivers. They must be at least twenty-one years old; be able to speak, read, and write English; pass a physical exam; have at least 20/40 vision with or without glasses; have good hearing; have a good driving record; and have at least one year's experience in truck driving.

Most long-haul truckers begin working at

local trucking jobs the way Joe did. Although truckers have a great deal of freedom and independence, the hours are long and tiring. Most truckers work at least fifty hours a week. The money they earn depends on the number of miles they have driven and the amount of time that they have spent away from home. These jobs can be hard to get.

Some truckers are *independent*. They work with many companies, and are paid for each job separately. They must pay for their own expenses and health benefits.

The salary range for all kinds of truckers is $15,000 to $40,000 a year. Most truckers who work for one company belong to unions and have paid health, holiday, sick day, retirement, and vacation benefits.

Other Careers in the Trucking Industry

Local truck drivers operate different sizes of trucks to deliver goods and materials within local areas.

These jobs require on-the-job training. There, drivers learn maintenance and operation procedures, routes, and how to do necessary paperwork. A high school diploma is preferred. The salary range is $17,000 to $25,000 a year.

Local and *long distance movers* move households, businesses, and materials both locally and across the country. They are responsible for loading, transporting, and unloading whatever cargo is being moved.

To be a mover, a high school diploma is preferred and good physical conditioning is essential. Movers are away from home for long periods of time. The salary range is $20,000 to $30,000 a year.

Shippers, *packers*, and *dock workers* pack, load, and unload freight. This job requires good common sense, judgment, and planning abilities. A high school diploma is preferred. The salary range is $15,000 to $25,000 a year. Training is mostly on-the-job.

Truck mechanics keep trucks running well. Mechanics who work for companies are responsible for the inspection, maintenance, and repairs of all company-owned vehicles. Mechanics usually work in a garage, but they also may repair trucks on the road.

A truck mechanic must have excellent mechanical skills. Some technical school training in truck mechanics is preferred, but on-the-job training is also available. The salary range is $20,000 to $30,000 a year.

Truck dispatchers coordinate the movement

of trucks entering and departing the truck terminal. They develop and coordinate schedules. They also maintain communication with drivers by phone or radio to ensure the safe arrival of the freight. The dispatcher is the main link with drivers who may be spread across the region or country.

Good organization, planning, and communication skills are necessary to be a dispatcher. Some college level training is useful. The salary range is $20,000 to $30,000.

Managers in the trucking industry are responsible for the administration and supervision of all activities and employees.

Management jobs usually require a four-year college degree. Good business, organization, planning, and communication skills are necessary to be successful in this job. The salary range is $40,000 to $60,000 a year.

Questions to Ask Yourself

Working in the trucking industry requires that you have several traits and skills. 1) What skills and traits do you need to enter the field of trucking? 2) Where can you learn to operate an eighteen-wheel truck? 3) What steps can you take to learn about truck mechanics?

Careers in the Automobile Industry

4

Of all the careers in the transportation field, those involved with the single family automobile may offer the most opportunities. The family car is almost a requirement in today's fast-paced society. Most families have at least two or even three cars.

With so many cars on the road, there are more and more job opportunities in manufacturing, assembly, sales, maintenance, driving instruction, parking, rentals, repair, licensing, inspections, and chauffeuring.

Judi, Future Taxi Driver

Judi was so excited when she got her driver's license. She loved to drive. Nothing compared to the freedom and excitement of driving.

She often used the family car to run errands for her parents and sisters. Neighbors asked Judi to drive them places when their cars were not available. She gained the reputation of being a safe and responsible driver.

In addition to being an excellent driver, Judi wanted to understand how cars worked. She decided to sign up for a course in auto mechanics to learn about car engines and maintenance. Her goal was to learn everything she could about cars. She wanted to get a job working with cars someday.

After researching various careers, Judi decided to become a taxi driver. This was a job where she could use both her driving and mechanical skills.

Taxi drivers, or cabbies, take passengers wherever they want to go. People are picked up at bus terminals, stations, airports, on city streets, and at individual homes. A taxi driver must know all of the roads and streets within a given area to be able to provide fast, efficient service. Taxi drivers also learn to operate a two-way cab radio. This is how the driver stays in contact with the *dispatcher*, the person who sends the taxi driver on job.

Taxi drivers must keep records of passenger destinations and collect *fares*, or money. Taxi drivers must be at least twenty-one years old, have a state-issued chauffeur's license, and a special taxi cab operator's license, which is issued by the Public Utilities Commission.

Cabbies usually earn 40 to 50 percent of their fares plus *tips*. A tip is money given by customers to cabbies for good service. The harder they work, the more they make. They often work long, twelve-hour days, five or six days a week. Cabbies can earn between $20,000 and $30,000 a year. Health, life insurance, and retirement benefits are usually provided by the company. Good driving skills and the ability to remain calm in heavy traffic are necessary. A high school diploma is preferred.

Other Careers in the Automobile Industry

There are many other exciting opportunities in this field. Young people with high school diplomas and some experience have a good chance of being hired in *entry level*, or beginning, positions. Many of these jobs offer some benefits, such as health insurance or paid sick or vacation days. Being ambitious and applying directly to personnel departments or shops may help you get the best jobs.

Chauffeurs drive people to specific locations in private cars or limousines. These drivers must be available at all times

Auto mechanics can take pride in knowing that their work helps keep their customers on the road and able to travel.

depending on the needs of the person or company that hires them.

To be a chauffeur, a high school diploma, a neat appearance, a chauffeur's license, and a good driving record are required. Wages are usually $5 to $10 an hour plus tips.

Parking lot attendants move and handle cars in private and public lots. They collect money, make change, and provide security for vehicles in lots. To be a parking lot attendant a driver's license is required, and a high school diploma is preferred. Wages are between $5 and $10 an hour.

Driving instructors teach new drivers how to drive. Instruction is given in a classroom and on the road.

Instructors are usually hired by driving schools, auto clubs, or community colleges. They must be good drivers who are patient and calm with people. A high school diploma is required. Wages are $10 to $15 an hour. For more information ask at your local auto club, community college, or driving school.

Auto mechanics inspect, repair, and service cars at service stations or car dealerships. As a mechanic, you will be exposed to dirt, dust, and fumes. Auto mechanics typically have a high school diploma. Specialized mechanical training at technical or trade schools may be helpful. Some mechanics learn on the job. Mechanics usually work forty hours a week and may work in *shifts*. A shift is either an eight- or twelve-hour period during the day or night. Wages are usually set at $10 to $20 an hour. Check with local service stations and car dealerships for job opportunities and requirements.

Car salespeople sell cars. They negotiate deals with customers to make a profit for the car dealership. They are also responsible for doing the necessary paperwork to close the deal. Hours can be long, and you may have to work in the evening.

A neat, clean appearance and good personal skills are required to be a car salesperson. Some college experience is suggested. Salaries are paid on *commission*, which means that you earn a percentage of the profit on any sale you make. A good salesperson can make a lot of money.

Car rental and *leasing agents* rent and lease cars at airports, railroad stations, bus terminals, and local city offices. They must know about rental requirements and how to do necessary paperwork. Some college experience may be preferred for this job. Computer training may be helpful. Good personal skills, since you will be working with the public, are necessay. The salary range is $15,000 to $20,000 a year.

Auto body repair workers repair the exterior, or body, of cars and trucks. They also repaint cars and do custom designs.

A high school diploma is preferred for auto body repair workers. Specialized training from a technical or trade school may be useful. On-the-job training may also be provided. Wages are $10 to $20 an hour. Check with local trade or technical schools for information on necessary training.

Factory auto workers assemble cars and trucks on production lines. They must possess some mechanical skills and be able to work well with others. They must be able to deal with repetitive tasks, since jobs are performed over and over during the course of the day. Jobs are done in shifts.

A high school diploma is preferred for factory auto workers. Most training is done on the job. Most jobs in automobile factories are unionized. That means that each of the employees must belong to a union. As you read earlier, a union is an organization that negotiates salaries, benefits, and working conditions for workers. The salary range is $15,000 to $25,000 a year.

Questions to Ask Yourself

The automobile industry is continually growing. You may find one or more careers that appeal to you in this field. 1) Do you think a driver's education or mechanic's course would help you in the future? Why or why not? 2) What type of jobs in the auto industry might be available immediately after high school? 3) Where can you learn more about auto careers that interest you?

Careers in Maritime Service

5

For some people, nothing compares to the sights, sounds, and smells of the open sea. These are the people for careers in the *maritime service*, or careers having to do with the sea.

Sherry, Future Seaman

Sherry's love of boats grew when her father bought a small fishing boat. She enjoyed keeping the boat in good condition.

Most weekends during the summer were spent boating and fishing. Sherry soon became good at repairing boat engines. She always seemed to know why an engine wouldn't work and how to fix it. This knowledge was useful when she applied for a summer job at a local marina.

Sherry got the job at the marina. She was excited about the variety of tasks that were part of her new job. She learned many new skills from other people who worked there. Her duties included doing minor repairs on boat engines, selling gas, oil, and groceries, and keeping watch on boats docked at the marina. She loved her summer job.

Sherry thought this might be a possible career for her. She enjoyed repairing engines and doing machine work. People at the marina were always asking for recommendations for a good boat mechanic to do major repairs. She decided that the possibilities sounded exciting and interesting.

After talking with several mechanics at other marinas, Sherry learned that most boat mechanics worked at larger marinas or indoor shops. In addition to working on engines, she wanted to travel and work her way up to better jobs. But there didn't seem to be much opportunity for either as a mechanic.

Sherry thought a position working on larger vessels, such as freighters, tankers, or passenger ships, would allow her to travel and move up the career ladder. She explored the available opportunities and decided to pursue a career as a seaman.

Seamen are actually both men and women. They are responsible for engine repair, storage and preparation of cargo and deck equipment. They also help with arrivals and departures, watch for objects in a ship's path, steer the ship, and perform general maintenance duties. Mechanical knowledge and ability are useful skills to have.

The government usually requires seafaring workers to obtain seamen's papers. These include a health certificate from a doctor, proof of citizenship, a passport photograph, and a written recommendation from a maritime training school or a ship's union.

Most seafaring jobs are obtained through unions. A person has to join a union to help her get available jobs. Competition for seamen jobs is tough. The salary range is $20,000 to $30,000 a year. Health, life insurance, and retirement benefits are offered to employees. Seamen may be away from home for long periods of time. But there are opportunities to travel all over the world.

Other Maritime Careers

Maritime careers offer many exciting opportunities. But some of these jobs require more education, training, and experience. Most of

Dock workers and longshoremen load and unload ships.

these jobs offer benefits such as health and life insurance and paid sick and vacation days. Many of these jobs are unionized.

Merchant marine radio officers are responsible for the operation, repair, and maintenance of radios aboard ships. They provide communication with other vessels and people on land.

To become radio officers, training and radio licensing through technical or training schools are required. The salary range is $20,000 to $30,000 a year.

Merchant marine captains and *officers* provide the leadership for operating a ship at sea. A four-year college degree is necessary to become a captain or officer. Specialized naval training at naval academies or coast guard facilities is required to understand and coordinate the operation of a large naval vessel. The salary range is $40,000 to $50,000 a year. The best way to begin this career is by contacting naval academies or coast guard facilities for more information.

Marina workers do a variety of jobs, including docking, refueling, providing weather information, giving advice on boating and safety procedures, and making minor repairs on boats.

Marina workers generally need a high school diploma. The salary range is $10,000 to $15,000 a year. Work is seasonal. You can apply in person at your local marina.

Dock workers, longshoremen and *car loaders* load and unload cargo at dock areas. Physical strength and endurance are necessary. Most of this work is outdoors and requires knowledge and operation of heavy machniery.

For these jobs, a high school diploma is preferred. On-the-job training is given to new employees. The salary range is $15,000 to $25,000 a year.

Merchant marine engineers are responsible

for the operation, repair, and maintenance of a ship's engines. Specialized mechanical training at a naval training school is needed to learn these skills. You will be required to work below deck for long periods of time. The salary range for merchant marine engineers is $25,000 to $30,000 a year.

Merchant marine pursers complete paperwork and other clerical tasks involved in the operation of a ship. Their duties include keeping records of the ship's accounts and payroll, and providing special services to passengers and crew. The salary range for pursers is $15,000 to $20,000 a year.

Commercial fishermen catch fish both night and day with large nets. They sell their catches to local restaurants and food companies.

This job involves long hours, hard physical work, and exposure to all types of weather. Wages are based on what fishermen are able to catch and sell. The range is usually $10,000 to $20,000 a year. On-the job training is provided.

Questions to Ask Yourself

There are many things to think about when you consider a maritime career. 1) Would you enjoy being away from home for long periods of time? 2) What type of high school courses might be helpful for a maritime career? 3) What kinds of boats would you like to work with?

Careers in Public Transit 6

The public transit system is run by individual cities. It provides transportation for the public. In most cities public transportation consists of buses and taxis. Some cities, such as New York, Chicago, and Washington, DC, have subways too. And some cities, such as San Francisco and New Orleans, have trolleys.

Andre, Future Bus Driver

Andre enjoyed riding the bus to school. The chance to drive a large bus with passengers seemed exciting and appealing to him.

Andre watched bus drivers closely as their buses glided along busy city streets. They used rear- and sideview mirrors to know exactly where traffic was around them. Andre saw that bus drivers had to be alert, responsible, and know local traffic situations in order to ensure the safety of their passengers.

When Andre was in high school, he went on a field trip to the public transit agency for the

Many people rely on public transportation. It is a necessary and important area of transportation to be a part of.

city. He was able to ride both the bus and subway systems and talk with different people in various jobs. Andre was convinced that a career as a bus driver was for him.

Bus drivers and *subway* and *trolley operators* pick up their buses or subway cars at the *terminals* where they are kept. They inspect them before beginning a trip.

Drivers must be familiar with the stops on their routes. Most bus, subway, or trolley drivers do not carry money and cannot give change. This is to limit the possibility of them being robbed.

Subway and trolley operators perform similar jobs. They must know how to operate track vehicles, as well as be alert to signals and lights along the route.

Drivers and operators must be at least twenty-one years old and in good physical condition. A high school diploma is preferred. A good driving record is essential. Most states require transit drivers and operators to have a special chauffeur's license. New workers are trained to drive a bus or operate a trolley or subway through classroom work and by operating the vehicle. They learn current rules and regulations for the job. All drivers must

Bus drivers can choose to work for a city bus company or one that provides
long distance travel.

then pass a written and operating exam to
obtain a commercial driver's license, or CDL.

Transit workers usually work in shifts. They
also may be required to work weekends or
holidays. Some may work a *swing shift*. This
means that they work for several hours in the
morning, have a long break, and then work
several hours more. Most drivers belong to a
union that negotiates their contract with the
transit system.

The ability to work with the public is a must.
Buses, subways, and trolleys run in all types of
weather. They are constantly involved in rush

hour traffic. Patience and good mechanical skills are good personal traits to have.

The salary range is $15,000 to $25,000 a year. Vacation days, health and life insurance, sick days, and retirement are some of the benefits drivers receive. Many drivers work their way up to supervisory positions. Supervisors make certain that buses and trolleys run on time.

Other Transit Careers

There are a variety of careers available within the transit system. Many of these jobs offer some benefits such as health and life insurance, retirement plans, and paid sick and vacation days.

School bus drivers transport students to and from school. They usually work swing shifts. They begin early in the morning and finish late in the afternoon. They may also drive students on field trips, sporting events, or special activities.

All school bus drivers must have a CDL, be in good physical condition, and possess a good driving record. Most drivers learn specifics about operating the bus through on-the-job training with experienced drivers. Wages are usually $5 to $7 an hour.

Special service bus drivers transport passengers to special locations. They may drive sightseeing and tour buses and provide tour information. Drivers also need to understand the mechanical operation of a bus, be knowledgeable about all safety procedures, and be able to make minor bus repairs.

This work may be full-time or part-time, as well as seasonal. On-the-job training is provided. Wages are usually $5 to $10 an hour. A CDL is required. Check with your local bus, tour, or transit company for more information.

Bus mechanics inspect, maintain and repair buses and their engines. Mechanics work primarily in bus garages, but sometimes they travel to repair disabled buses.

Bus mechanics usually have a high school diploma. Knowledge about bus engines can be learned through technical schools. Some training is on-the-job. Wages are set at $5 to $10 an hour. A CDL is usually required.

Bus dispatchers are responsible for the arrival and departure of buses from a terminal. They stay in contact with drivers to answer questions or solve problems that drivers may have along the route. Most dispatchers begin their careers as drivers. A high school diploma is preferred, as well as a CDL. Wages usually begin at $8 to $15 an hour.

Bus ticket agents sell tickets and handle luggage. They provide information and assistance to passengers. Agents may have salaries or work for an hourly rate. The salary range is $15,000 to $25,000 a year.

Subway token booth clerks sell tokens for the subway. They also offer information about and maps of the subway system to travelers. Clerks may be paid a salary or an hourly wage. The salary range is $15,000 to $25,000 a year.

Managers oversee the company's workers and perform executive duties. A four-year college degree is usually required to be a manager, but some people may be promoted from jobs as drivers or mechanics. The salary range is $30,000 to $50,000 a year.

Clerical workers keep track of records, personnel, and forms that must be completed during the course of the working day.

For clerical workers, a high school diploma is preferred. Business, computer, or clerical experience are all useful in getting a job in this field. Wages are usually $7 to $10 an hour.

Questions to Ask Yourself

Each state has a different public transit authority with different requirements. 1) What jobs require a commercial driver's license (CDL)? 2) What are the public transit organizations in your area? 3) Would you mind working swing shifts?

Preparing for a Career in Transportation

7

The transportation industry is growing because of the need for reliable and efficient transportation. Many people apply for transportation jobs, so the competition can be tough. If you are seriously considering a career in transportation, there are many ways you can prepare yourself while in high school. Employers look for people who will do a good job and make a positive impression on customers. To do this, you must have good writing, speaking, and grooming skills. These can set you apart from hundreds of other job applicants.

Writing Skills

The ability to express yourself in writing is essential. Good communication skills in letter writing and other forms of written expression often make a person stand out.

Learning how to write and type a *résumé* is necessary. A résumé is a written summary of a person's background and experience. Employers often ask for a résumé to learn about your present job goals and past job experiences. You can refer to the book about writing résumés in the For Further Reading section on page 62.

When you send your résumé to a possible employer, you must also send a *cover letter*. A cover letter offers a brief introduction. It should mention where you learned of the job opportunity, your basic qualifications, why you think you are a good candidate for the job, and a request for an interview. There must be no errors in grammar, spelling, or sentence structure. Ask your teacher, guidance counselor, or parents for help in writing such a letter. You can also check a book out at the library on writing cover letters.

Speaking Skills

People in the transportation field must also have good speaking skills because, as a service industry, employees deal directly with people. Being patient, polite, and helpful suggests a willingness to communicate positively with others. Much of this takes practice and common sense.

Most people will have a job *interview* to meet their potential employer face to face. The interview will give you a chance to express yourself and learn more about the job. It also gives the employer an opportunity to see how you relate and talk with people.

Ask your guidance counselor to help you prepare for an interview. Courses in public speaking may help to improve your communication skills. You can practice interviewing with friends and family.

Grooming Skills

Besides writing and speaking skills, the way you dress says a lot about you. First impressions are important. The first thing an employer will notice about you is your appearance. If you are neat and well groomed, you will make a good impression.

If you are unsure about what to wear to interviews, ask your parents or school counselor for their opinions. Listen to their advice. They have had experience with interviews and may be able to give you some valuable tips.

Power, responsibility, and independence are three reasons to go into the field of transportation. Freedom, world travel, and excitement are three more. If you find any of these things interesting, consider a career in transportation. When you realize how many years a person spends working, you will understand that it pays to go into something that you really enjoy. Transportation offers many careers. Perhaps one of them is for you.

Questions to Ask Yourself

Writing, speaking, and grooming are important skills to consider in applying for and getting a job. 1) How can you learn to write a good résumé? 2) How good are your writing, speaking, and grooming skills? 3) How can you improve them?

Glossary

benefits   Money or other services given to employees of an organization.

cabbie   Slang term for a taxi-driver.

CDL   Abbreviation for *Commercial Driver's License.*

interview   Meeting with a possible employer.

license   Permission given by the law to do a specific job.

marina   Dock for anchoring boats.

promotion   To obtain a higher level job.

résumé   Written summary of career goals, experiences, skills, and abilities.

rig   Truck designed to pull heavy loads.

seniority   Term based on age, position, or length of service.

shift   Time period of work.

swing shift   Working for several hours, followed by a long break and then a return to work.

union   Group of workers united to protect interests and rights of members.

wages or **salary**   Money paid to employees to perform a job.

For More Information

Here are lists of places to obtain further information about careers in the transportation industry.

United Transportation
  Union
14600 Detroit Avenue
Lakewood, OH 44107
(216) 228-9400

Airline Careers

Airline Pilots'
  Association
1625 Massachusetts
  Avenue NW
Washington, DC
  20036
(202) 797-4033

Association of Flight
  Attendants
1625 Massachusetts
  Avenue NW
Washington, DC 20036
(202) 328-5400

Automobile Industry

Automobile Service
  Association, Inc.
P.O. Box 929
Bedford, TX 76021-0929
(817) 283-6205

National Automobile
  Transporters
  Association
(313) 965-6533

National Automotive
  Technicians Education
  Foundation
13505 Dulles Technology
  Drive
Hearndon, VA 22071-
  3415
(703) 713-0100

Maritime Industry

National Maritime
  Union
346 17th Street
New York, NY 10011
(212) 614-6600

Seafarers' International
  Union
5201 Auth Way
Camp Spring, MD 20746
(301) 899-0675

Public Transit

American Bus
  Association
1015 15th Street NW
Washington, DC 20005
(202) 842-1645

American Public Transit
  Association
1201 New York Avenue
  NW
Washington, DC 20005
(202) 898-4000

Rail Careers

Brotherhood of
  Locomotive
  Engineers
1365 Ontario Street
Cleveland, OH 44114
(216) 241-2630

Brotherhood of Railroad
  Signalmen
601 West Golf Road
Mt. Prospect, IL 60056
(847) 439-3732

Trucking Industry

American Trucking
  Association, Inc.
2200 Mill Road
Alexandria, VA 22314
(703) 838-1880

Professional Truck
  Driver Institute of
  America
8788 Elk Grove
  Boulevard
Elk Grove, CA 95624
(916) 686-5146

For Further Reading

Carter, Sharon. *Careers in Aviation*.
New York: Rosen Publishing Group,
1990.

*Encyclopedia of Career and Vocational
Guidance*. Chicago: J. G. Ferguson
Publishing Co., 1990.

Grant, Edgar. *Exploring Careers in the Travel
Industry*. New York: Rosen Publishing
Group, 1989.

Green, George. *Some Say It Couldn't Have
Happened to a Nicer Fella*. Victoria, B.C.:
Conway Publishing Co., 1995.

Lobus, Catherine Okray. *Careers as a Flight
Attendant,* rev. ed. New York: Rosen
Publishing Group, 1996.

Occupational Outlook Handbook.
Washington, DC: Bureau of Labor Statistics,
U. S. Department of Labor, 1995.

Schauer, Donald D. *Careers in Trucking*. New
York: Rosen Publishing Group, 1991.

Index

About the Author
Bruce McGlothlin is a school psychologist/counselor employed by the Allegheny Intermediate Unit in Pittsburgh, Pennsylvania. He holds graduate degrees in both school psychology and counseling. He is the author of several books and games for young adults including *Traveling Light*, *Great Grooming for Guys*, *Search and Succeed*, *High Performance Through Understanding Systems* and "The Academic/Feeling Trivia Game".

Bruce and his wife, Judi, are the parents of two teenage children, Michael and Molly. His hobbies are running, biking, snowshoeing, reading, watch and fountain pen collecting, and jigsaw puzzles.

Photo Credits: Cover © T. Maitie/Impact Visuals; p. 2 © Ken Martin/Impact Visuals; pp. 7, 24, 36 © Jim West/Impact Visuals; p. 10 © Earl Dotter/Impact Visuals; pp. 13, 50 © F. M. Kearney/Impact Visuals; p. 15 © Alain McLaughlin/Impact Visuals; p. 20 © Michael Kaufman/Impact Visuals; p. 29 © Slobodan Dimitrou/Impact Visuals; p. 43 © Laurie ▉ek/Impact Visuals; p. 48 by Michael Brandt.

▉n: Erin McKenna